ENERGY
Now and in the Future

Fossil Fuels

Neil Morris

A+
Smart Apple Media

Smart Apple Media
P.O. Box 3263
Mankato, MN 56002

Printed in the United States of America

Library of Congress Cataloging-in-Publication Data

Morris, Neil, 1946-
  Fossil fuels / by Neil Morris.
      p. cm. -- (Energy now and in the future)
  Includes bibliographical references and index.
  Summary: "Discusses how fossil fuels are used for energy, how the environmental
impact of fossil fuels could be reduced, and ways fossil fuels could be used in the
future"--Provided by publisher.
  ISBN 978-1-59920-339-3 (hardcover : alk. paper)
  1. Fossil fuels--Juvenile literature. I. Title.
  TP318.3.M674 2010
  333.8'2--dc22
                                                            2008043226

Designed by Helen James
Edited by Mary-Jane Wilkins
Artwork by Guy Callaby
Picture research by Su Alexander

Photograph acknowledgements
Page 7 Remi Benali/Corbis; 11 Kazuyoshi Nomachi/Corbis; 12 Historical Picture
Archive/Corbis; 14 David Mdzinarishvili/Reuters/Corbis; 17 Chinch Gryniewicz/
Ecoscene/Corbis; 18 Bob Fleumer/Zefa/Corbis; 19 Larry Lee Photography/Corbis;
20 Claudius/Zefa/Corbis; 22 Fabian Cevallos/Corbis Sygma; 23 Corbis; 25 Tim
Wright/Corbis; 27 Patrick Pleul/dpa/Corbis; 28 Brownie Harris/Corbis; 31 Ed Kashi/
Corbis; 32 Klaus Leidorf/Zefa/Corbis; 35 Ladislav Janicek/Zefa/Corbis; 36 Daniel J
Cox/Corbis; 37 Galen Rowell/Corbis; 38 Marco Simoni/Robert Harding World
Imagery/Corbis; 42 NASA/Corbis
Front cover David Mdzinarishvili/Reuters/Corbis

9 8 7 6 5 4 3 2 1

Contents

Prehistoric Energy

The world's main fossil fuels are coal, oil, and natural gas. They are called fossil fuels because all three substances were formed from the fossilized remains of prehistoric organic matter—either plants or animals. People have been burning coal, oil, and gas as fuel for many centuries.

Coal, oil, and gas are hydrocarbons—compounds of the chemical elements hydrogen and carbon. They burn well in air and give off energy in the form of heat. These types of fuel have served us well in the past, but this may change in the future. Because fossil fuels give off a gas called carbon dioxide when they burn, scientists believe that this has an enormous effect on our planet by warming it up and changing our climate (see pages 38–39).

Crushed for Centuries

Fossil fuels began to form more than 3 billion years ago. The early oceans were full of simple organisms—tiny, single-celled plants and animals, such as blue-green algae. When these microscopic organisms died, their remains sank to the seabed. The organic remains were soon covered by fine-grained mud and sand sediments, which buried and preserved them. Over time, the organic matter formed layers, as more dead plants and animals sank. Each layer was then compressed by the weight of new layers on top, which also produced heat. The combination of pressure and heat caused the sediments to turn into rock such as sandstone (called sedimentary rock), and the organic matter changed into a waxy substance that we call kerogen.

Solid, Liquid, and Gas

The three main fossil fuels take different forms. Coal is a solid rock. There are many types of coal, ranging from a soft brown rock to a much harder black one. Crude oil (also called petroleum) is a sticky liquid that can be refined into many different liquid and gaseous fuels. Natural gas is, of course, gaseous and it is called natural to distinguish it from coal gas, which was first made by heating coal in the seventeenth century.

Crude oil is generally a dark brown color, though it may be a lighter shade or even black. It is about 85 percent carbon and 12 percent hydrogen, along with traces of other substances.

Forming Oil and Gas

At a certain depth and temperature—generally deeper than 2,500 feet (760 m) and at a temperature of about 212°F (100°C)—kerogen separated into a liquid (oil) and a gas (natural gas). As more time passed, the weight of the overlying layers forced the oil and gas upward through cracks in the sedimentary rock. Water, which is denser than oil, also pushed the oil upward. This upward movement continued until the oil and gas reached a layer of impermeable rock, which had no cracks or holes. This trapped the oil and gas underground.

Why Are Fossil Fuels Nonrenewable?

They are called nonrenewable because they take thousands (or even millions) of years to form, and we are taking fossil fuels out of the ground all the time. This continually reduces the overall stock of these fuels as we use them faster than they can form. Once the present stocks are all used, there will be no more fossil fuels. That is why people all over the world are taking much more interest in renewable sources of energy. These include biomass, water, wind, geothermal, and solar energy.

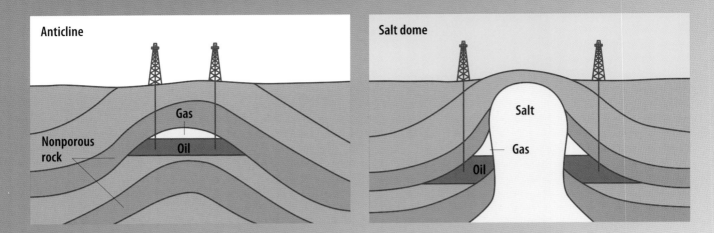

Trapped Oil

While fossil fuels were forming, Earth's surface was changing. Movements in Earth's crust raised areas of the seabed above the ocean. These became land. The movements also bent and cracked layers of rock, trapping oil. When oil is trapped, it forms a reservoir or pocket. Oil floats to the top of water and natural gas bubbles to the top of oil, so many oil reservoirs have a layer of natural gas on top. Two of the most common forms of oil traps are anticlines and salt domes.

An anticline is an arch-shaped formation of sedimentary rock layers created by movements in Earth's crust. Oil and gas become trapped beneath the arch of nonporous rock. A salt dome traps oil and gas in the same way. This formation is caused by salt deposits moving up through overlying rocks.

Anticlines and salt domes trap oil and gas underground. Once geologists have found these features, engineers drill down to release the fossil fuels.

The Forests that Turned into Coal

Coal formed from larger, more complicated plants that grew in swampy forests. Most of these plants began to form during a time we call the Carboniferous Period, sometimes known as the Age of Coal Forests. This lasted from about 360 to 286 million years ago. Dead giant ferns and other tree-like plants fell into the warm, shallow water of the swamps. The dead vegetation on the forest floor was soon covered by more organic matter, which pressed the layers tightly together. Over a long period of time, pressure and increasing heat began to change the organic material.

The amount of carbon in the matter increased, while the amount of hydrogen and oxygen decreased. This turned it into a spongy mass called peat. At the same time, other mineral matter turned into sedimentary rocks such as sandstone and shale.

Soft and Hard Coals

The increasing weight of the vegetable and mineral layers changed the peat into a dry, crumbly substance called lignite (from the Latin word for wood). Lignite is also known as brown coal because of its color. As the pressure continued to increase with more layers and greater depth, the lignite became subbituminous coal (from the Latin word bitumen, a kind of tarry pitch). As it became harder and drier, it turned into bituminous coal and finally into the hardest coal of all—anthracite (from the Greek word for coal). Anthracite is sometimes simply called hard coal. It has the highest carbon content and the least moisture of all the different kinds of coal.

How Much Coal Is Left and Where?

The World Coal Institute says: "Coal reserves are available in almost every country worldwide, with recoverable reserves in around 70 countries. At current production levels, proven coal reserves are estimated to last 147 years." That means no more coal after 2155. The pie chart shows the countries with the largest coal reserves (and their percentage of world reserves).

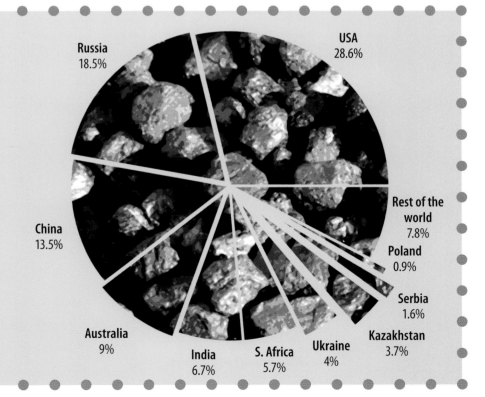

Russia 18.5%

USA 28.6%

Rest of the world 7.8%

Poland 0.9%

Serbia 1.6%

Kazakhstan 3.7%

Ukraine 4%

S. Africa 5.7%

India 6.7%

Australia 9%

China 13.5%

Power through the Centuries

Coal, gas, and oil have played an important part in human history. Along with wood, which is a form of biomass, fossil fuels have been used for heating, cooking, powering vehicles and other machines, and for generating electricity.

Ancient Days of Coal

Archaeologists have found evidence that people burned coal in northern Europe up to 4,000 years ago. Some Chinese experts believe that their ancestors burned coal as fuel even earlier—up to 10,000 years ago. We know that by about 300 B.C., ancient Chinese metalworkers were burning coal to smelt copper.

Most of the coal used in ancient times must have come from outcrops that had been exposed by movements in Earth's surface, which made it easy to dig it out of the ground. Eventually, people started digging further downward, creating the first mines. The Italian traveler Marco Polo (1254–1324) described seeing people digging "black stones" out of the mountains of northern China. Once lit, the stones burned throughout the night and gave off great heat. The stones were clearly lumps of coal.

Worshipping Eternal Fires

Natural gas was also discovered by the ancient Chinese when they dug wells to collect underground brine (salty water) more than 2,000 years ago.

Aristotle's Burning Rocks

The ancient Greek philosopher and scientist Aristotle (384–322 B.C.) mentioned coal in his book *Meteorologica*, about earth sciences. Referring to rocks that could catch fire, Aristotle mentioned coal-like substances and called them "bodies which have more of earth than of smoke." Theophrastus (372–287 B.C.), Aristotle's pupil in Athens, also recorded the use of coal in ancient Greece.

The Chinese allowed the gas to flow through bamboo pipes and then lit it to heat pans of brine, so that it boiled and produced salt. In western Asia, near the Caspian Sea, people began worshipping at temples with "eternal fires" during the sixth century A.D. The Zoroastrian fire-worshippers thought the fires were the result of a miracle and had divine power. In fact, the temple flames were produced by lighting the natural methane gas that escaped from under ground through cracks in the earth.

This sacred flame has been burning in a Zoroastrian fire temple in central Iran for at least 1,500 years.

Is China the Coal Giant of the World?

From ancient times to the seventeenth century, China was probably the world's largest producer and consumer of coal. The Industrial Revolution in Europe and North America did not occur in China. Compare the figures for the beginning of the twentieth and twenty-first centuries. China is again the largest producer of coal. By contrast, the United Kingdom (UK), which was in second place in 1905, produced just 18.5 megatons (millions of metric tons or Mt) in 2006.

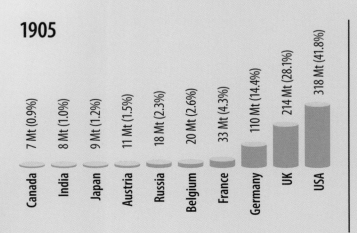

1905

Canada	India	Japan	Austria	Russia	Belgium	France	Germany	UK	USA
7 Mt (0.9%)	8 Mt (1.0%)	9 Mt (1.2%)	11 Mt (1.5%)	18 Mt (2.3%)	20 Mt (2.6%)	33 Mt (4.3%)	110 Mt (14.4%)	214 Mt (28.1%)	318 Mt (41.8%)

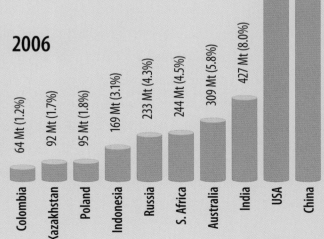

2006

Colombia	Kazakhstan	Poland	Indonesia	Russia	S. Africa	Australia	India	USA	China
64 Mt (1.2%)	92 Mt (1.7%)	95 Mt (1.8%)	169 Mt (3.1%)	233 Mt (4.3%)	244 Mt (4.5%)	309 Mt (5.8%)	427 Mt (8.0%)	990 Mt (18.4%)	2482 Mt (46.2%)

This early locomotive, Puffing Billy, was built in 1813. It hauled coal from a mine to the docks in northeast England. It traveled at a top speed of 5 miles (8 km) per hour.

Steaming Ahead

The Industrial Revolution began in Britain in the eighteenth century. The two great power sources were wind and water. The invention of the steam engine changed everything, and soon steam—created by burning coal to heat water—was driving machines in factories and mines throughout the country and later the world.

English engineer Thomas Savery (1650–1715) invented the first practical steam engine in 1698 to pump water from mines. Fourteen years later, Thomas Newcomen (1663–1729) developed a more efficient steam pump that had a cylinder fitted with a piston. In 1769, James Watt (1736–1819) made further improvements with an engine that used less coal and produced more power. Watt's engine used a condenser to change steam back into water. In 1782, he improved it by developing a double-action machine that used steam to push a piston both ways.

Iron Smelting

English ironmaster Abraham Darby (1678–1717) wanted to make iron cheaper and easier to produce. His furnace burned charcoal, made from wood, which was becoming scarce in early eighteenth-century England. So in 1709, Darby converted his furnace to burn a fuel called coke instead of charcoal. Coke was made from coal by heating it in an airtight oven. The new furnace was ideal for smelting iron. Along with coal and steam, iron became a vital element in the Industrial Revolution.

New Locomotives

In 1804, English engineer Richard Trevithick (1771–1833) built a steam engine to pull wagons in an ironworks. Ten years later, George Stephenson (1781–1848) designed and built a steam locomotive to run on rails and haul coal from mines. Stephenson then constructed the Stockton and Darlington Railway. In 1829, his son Robert Stephenson (1803–59) helped him build an improved locomotive, which pulled a special train to open the Liverpool and Manchester Railway a year later. The new engine was called Rocket. It pulled its own coal and water in a tender. It could travel at 28.5 miles (46 km) per hour—incredibly fast for the time.

Is Coal-Produced Steam Important Today?

Steam engines are not used much today, although steam-driven locomotives still pull trains in some parts of the world. But coal-powered steam turbines are still used almost everywhere to generate electricity (see page 25). The world's first coal-fired power station opened on Pearl Street, New York, in 1882 and was used for lighting. Today, many countries still produce more than half their electricity by coal.

Coal Gas

When coal is heated to about 2000° F (1100°C) in an airtight oven, it gives off hydrogen and methane in the form of coal gas. This was first done in Flanders in the early seventeenth century. Then, in 1792, the British engineer William Murdoch (1754–1839), who worked for James Watt, succeeded in lighting his home with gas that he made from coal. A few years later, the new invention was used to light cotton mills. In 1807, the first gaslights lit the streets of London. This innovation was very popular. By 1819, there were more than 280 miles (450 km) of gas pipes in the English capital.

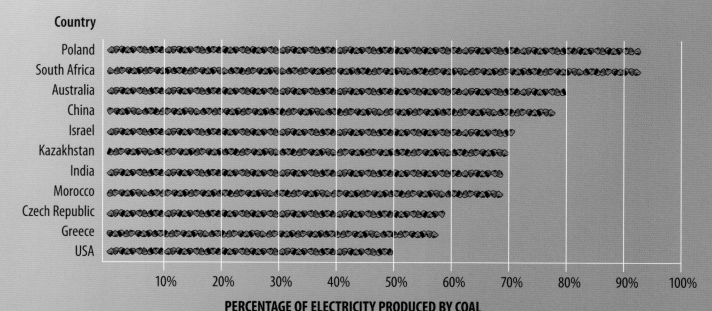

Country

Poland									
South Africa									
Australia									
China									
Israel									
Kazakhstan									
India									
Morocco									
Czech Republic									
Greece									
USA									

10% 20% 30% 40% 50% 60% 70% 80% 90% 100%

PERCENTAGE OF ELECTRICITY PRODUCED BY COAL

Fountains of Pitch

Archaeologists have found evidence of an ancient oil seep near the Euphrates River in Mesopotamia (modern Iraq). They believe that locals gathered asphalt (oily tar) at these "fountains of pitch," as they were known. They probably used the pitch to waterproof baskets, boats, and baths. It may also have been used to hold stones together in the walls and towers of the ancient city of Babylon.

There were small oil springs in many other parts of the world, too. By the fourth century A.D., the Chinese had begun to dig oil wells, mainly when searching for brine and salt. Six hundred years later, the Arab geographer al-Masudi described seeing oil fields near Baku, in present-day Azerbaijan. But it was not until the nineteenth century that explorers and engineers began to look seriously at the possibility of recovering large quantities of oil.

Oil derricks and pumps line the coast of the Caspian Sea near Baku, the capital of Azerbaijan. This region is still important for the production of oil and natural gas.

How the Nobel Prizes Are Funded

In 1879, Alfred Nobel (1833–96) set up an oil company in Baku, then in the Russian Empire, with his two older brothers and family friend Peter Bilderling (1844–1900). The company made so much money that five years later it was worth five times as much. Alfred Nobel made even more money from his greatest invention—dynamite. In his will he left a huge sum to fund Nobel Prizes for chemistry, literature, medicine, peace, and physics. These world-famous prizes are still awarded every year.

Black Gold

In 1859, a retired railway conductor named Edwin Drake (1819–80) took over some oil pits near Titusville in Pennsylvania. People had already been drilling for oil here and elsewhere, but Drake had a new idea. As he drilled down using the power of a steam engine, he lined the drill hole with an iron pipe so that it did not collapse and fill with earth or water. Drake drilled down to the bedrock at about 70 feet (21 m)—and struck oil! Soon he and his men were filling old wooden whiskey barrels with "black gold."

When Will Oil and Gas Run Out?

According to the U.S. *World Factbook 2008*, the world is using 80 million barrels of oil and 11,000 cubic yards (8,300 cu m) of gas a day. Proven oil and gas reserves show that, if consumption stayed at this level and no more reserves were found, oil would last for another 44 years (until 2052) and gas would last another 57 years (until 2065). Other sources believe the gas may last a bit longer—up to 72 years. Optimists hope that we may find further reserves before the fuels run out. Experts currently believe that more than half the world's oil reserves are in Saudi Arabia, Canada, Iran, and Iraq, and that more than half the gas is in Russia, Iran, and Qatar (see page 19).

Oil Barrels

The standard measure used for oil is the barrel, which holds 42 gallons (159 L). Early U.S. oil producers filled old 40 gallon (151 L) whiskey barrels, as they were easy to find. But the Standard Oil Company, founded in 1870, always shipped its oil in 42 gallon (159 L) barrels, to allow for evaporation and leakage. This soon became the standard measure everywhere.

Mining and Refining

Fossil fuels are all underground, so we have to extract them before we can use them. Coal is mined; oil and natural gas are obtained by drilling. Oil and gas have to be processed and refined before being burned as fuel. Mining and refining technologies have improved in recent decades, but the basic processes remain the same.

Coal at the Surface

Like other sedimentary rocks, coal lies in layers beneath the surface of Earth. The coal layers (or seams) can be up to 328 feet (100 m) wide. Some lie horizontally, separated by layers of other rocks, but many have been bent and folded by underground movements and the formation of mountains. Horizontal seams near the surface are often covered by rocks and soil—called an overburden—that can be removed in an open-pit mine. Mining engineers may use explosives to break up the solid surface and then remove the overburden with digging machines.

Digging Deeper

The deepest coal mines have vertical shafts. Miners and equipment are lowered down through a shaft, and the coal is carried up to the surface through another shaft.

Chinese Disasters

China has had many coal-mining disasters over the years. More than 1,500 miners died in an accident in Japanese-occupied Manchuria in 1942. During 2004, about 6,000 Chinese miners were killed in different accidents. On February 14, 2005, an earthquake shook a deep mine in Fuxin. Ten minutes later, there was a gas explosion 793 feet (242 m) underground. At least 214 miners were killed. This and other blasts may have been caused by poor ventilation in deep mines.

This hillside coal face and open-pit mine in South Wales was a major coal-mining region through the nineteenth and much of the twentieth century.

There are two main methods of cutting coal. The traditional method is called room-and-pillar. Horizontal tunnels lead from the main shafts and the coal is dug out in spaces called rooms. Many modern mines use the longwall method. This cuts coal from one long part of the coal face with a powerful shearing machine. Steel props support the roof over the face while the coal is being cut. This method uses fewer miners and is generally more productive.

Is Mining Bad for the Environment?

Both surface and underground coal mining can harm the environment. Open-pit mines leave large areas of scarred land, although many companies now reclaim and improve mined land. Deep mines can cause land to sink and are dangerous for a long time after the mine is closed. Mine waste (called tailings) can seep into waterways and pollute them. The environmental group Friends of the Earth comments on the damage done to the environment by mining: "Open-pit mining...has a devastating impact on local communities and their environment, as companies strive to produce ever cheaper coal. However, the cost is high for the thousands of people who have to live with the consequences of environmental degradation, pollution, noise, and falling house prices. Friends of the Earth is calling on the government to tackle the problem and change planning policy in favor of the communities who are victims of this runaway industry."

Exploring for Oil and Gas

Companies extract oil and gas by drilling down to the pockets that hold them. They once relied on a mixture of guesswork and luck, but today's oil surveyors use advanced scientific equipment. First, they identify promising sites from aerial and satellite photographs. Then, they use instruments to work out what is beneath the ground or the seabed. A gravimeter (gravity meter) measures differences in the underground pull of gravity, giving information about rocks. A magnetometer measures changes in the magnetic field. Thumper trucks create underground vibrations that can be measured by seismographs to show faults where there may be pockets of oil and gas.

Offshore oil and gas rigs can be reached by boat and helicopter. The sea is calm in this photograph, but rigs must be able to withstand severe storms.

Derricks and Drills

When a company finds oil, it builds the steel framework—called a derrick—that holds the drilling equipment. If the site is beneath the ocean, the derrick sits on a large platform that forms part of a rig. In shallow water near the coast, the rig may stand on legs on the seabed. In deeper water, floating rigs have vast buoyancy tanks to keep them afloat and stable. The platforms include living quarters for the workers and a landing pad for the helicopters that carry them to and from shore.

Spinning Bits

Sharp-toothed bits drill down through the rocks to oil and gas pockets. The bits are attached to the end of a series of linked steel pipes. Mud is pumped down the pipes to keep the bit cool and clean. Oil rig workers called roughnecks change the bit and add sections of pipe when necessary. This is hard, dangerous work.

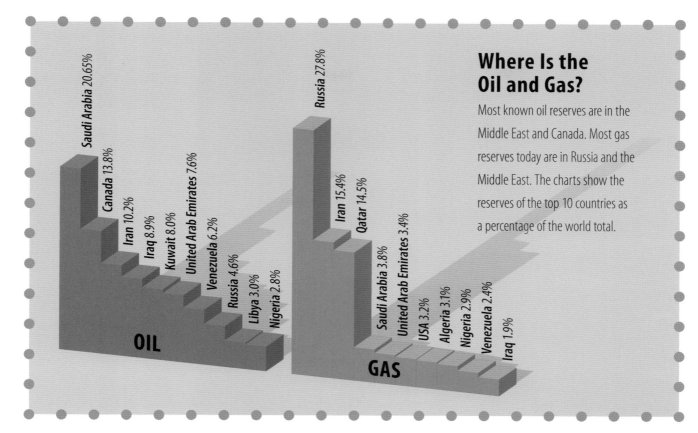

Where Is the Oil and Gas?

Most known oil reserves are in the Middle East and Canada. Most gas reserves today are in Russia and the Middle East. The charts show the reserves of the top 10 countries as a percentage of the world total.

OIL

Saudi Arabia 20.65%
Canada 13.8%
Iran 10.2%
Iraq 8.9%
Kuwait 8.0%
United Arab Emirates 7.6%
Venezuela 6.2%
Russia 4.6%
Libya 3.0%
Nigeria 2.8%

GAS

Russia 27.8%
Iran 15.4%
Qatar 14.5%
Saudi Arabia 3.8%
United Arab Emirates 3.4%
USA 3.2%
Algeria 3.1%
Nigeria 2.9%
Venezuela 2.4%
Iraq 1.9%

When the drill has almost reached the oil pocket, tubing is lowered into the drill hole and a small explosion blasts away the last pieces of rock. In wells with enough natural pressure, oil then gushes up the tubing and is controlled by a set of valves on the rig platform. If there is not enough pressure, water or steam is injected into the oil pocket down a separate tube to pump the oil to the surface. There is often natural gas on top of oil deposits or dissolved in them, so the gas is usually recovered at the same time.

Roughnecks (oil workers) use a huge wrench to operate and change drill pipes at the turntable of an oil platform.

This modern refinery at Leuna, in eastern Germany, can process 225,000 barrels of oil per day.

Off to the Refinery

Crude oil has to go to a refinery to be turned into petroleum products we can use. Some oil is pumped through long pipelines, such as the 808 mile (1,300 km) long Trans-Alaska Pipeline from the Arctic to the Pacific coast. This pipeline is about 4 feet (1.2 m) wide. More than a million barrels of crude oil are pumped through it every day, taking nine days to complete the journey. At the port of Valdez, the oil is stored in vast tanks before being transferred to tanker ships for delivery to refineries.

The world's largest oil tankers are massive ships known as ultra large crude carriers (ULCCs). Each ULCC can carry more than 330,000 tons (300,000 t) of cargo; the largest is 1,502 feet (458 m) long and holds more than 4 million barrels of oil. This ship, the *Knock Nevis*, was built in Japan and is owned by Norwegians. It is now a floating storage and offloading unit near the Qatar oil fields off the coast of the Persian Gulf.

What Happens at the Refinery

At the refinery, crude oil is changed by heat into various mixtures of hydrocarbons. The oil is heated by a furnace to 752°F (400°C) before passing into a tall steel column called a fractionating tower. The tower is hottest at the bottom and coolest at the top. The various oils and gases boil and condense at different temperatures. Groups of hydrocarbons with high boiling points condense first and flow out near the bottom of the tower. Groups such as butane and propane have such low boiling points that they do not condense at all, but remain as gases.

Cracking

The refinery uses heat, pressure, and chemicals to change one combination of hydrocarbons into another. Many processes help to produce more petroleum from a barrel of oil. One of these is cracking, which breaks down—or cracks—heavier fractions into lighter ones. The process improves the quality of petroleum by making it a higher octane number (octane is a liquid hydrocarbon). This means it burns more smoothly in an engine.

Oil Top 10

These figures show oil production in thousands of barrels a day and each country's percentage of the world total. The top 10 countries produce two-thirds of the world's oil.

Country	Production	World %
Saudi Arabia	11,100	14.1
Russia	9,870	12.5
USA	8,322	10.6
Iran	4,150	5.3
Mexico	3,784	4.8
China	3,710	4.7
Canada	3,092	3.9
Norway	2,978	3.8
Venezuela	2,802	3.6
Kuwait	2,669	3.4

What Comes from a Barrel of Crude?

The most important product is gasoline. More than one-third of the world's crude oil is refined into gasoline. Other main products are distillate fuel oil (mainly diesel oil) and jet fuel (mainly kerosene). The image shows the products obtained from a barrel of crude oil in California.

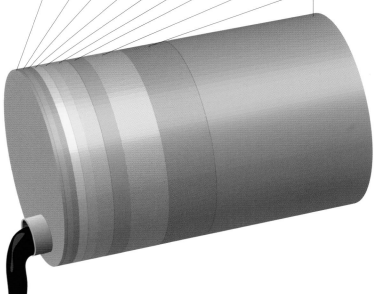

Lubricants 0.9%
Other refined products 1.5%
Asphalt and road oil 1.7%
Liquefied refinery gas 2.8%
Residual fuel oil 3.3%
Marketable coke 5.0%
Still gas 5.4%
Jet fuel 12.3%
Distillate fuel oil 15.3%
Gasoline 51.4%

FOSSIL FUELS

The Trans-Siberian gas pipeline must survive severe winters. It is 2,800 miles (4,500 km) long.

Delivering Gas

Natural gas is collected through small gathering systems. It is sent through pipelines to gas processing plants (or refineries) to remove impurities from the gas. The gathering lines move natural gas to large transmission pipelines. There are approximately 280,000 miles (445,000 km) of natural gas transmission pipelines throughout the world, both onshore and offshore.

New Pipelines

Engineers plan to build new pipelines to carry natural gas across tough terrain, such as northern Canada, Siberia, and the Sahara. There are plans to build the longest natural gas pipeline across 5,000 miles (8,000 km) of South American wilderness. The Gasoducto del Sur (Southern Gas Pipeline) would connect the gas fields of Venezuela to Argentina. But it would have to cross Brazil's Amazon rainforest, and environmentalists believe it could threaten the natural habitat and local cultures.

Long gas pipelines also are being built across the ocean floor. The Langeled pipeline has tens of thousands of individual steel sections. When complete, it will stretch 745 miles (1,200 km) from the Ormen Lange field off the coast of Norway to Easington, on the eastern coast of England.

Gas Top 10

Natural gas production in billions of cubic yards (cu m) a year. The top four countries produce half the world's gas.

Country	Production	World %
Russia	858.3 (656.2)	23.2
USA	641.9 (490.8)	17.3
Canada	233.1 (178.2)	6.3
Iran	132.1 (101.0)	3.6
Algeria	110.4 (84.4)	3.0
UK	110.1 (84.2)	3.0
Norway	109.1 (83.4)	2.9
Netherlands	98.9 (75.6)	2.7
Indonesia	96.8 (74.0)	2.6
Saudi Arabia	89.3 (68.3)	2.4

Is Natural Gas Dangerous?

The main hydrocarbon in natural gas is methane, the lightest hydrocarbon. There are also small amounts of ethane, propane, butane, and pentane that are dangerous to breathe. Because natural gas has little or no smell, gas companies add a chemical to make it smell. This helps people notice leaks from pipes or gas coming from appliances such as stoves that are turned on but not lit. Gas is explosive, so pipelines can be dangerous.

In 1989, two trains passing in opposite directions near a leaking gas pipeline in Russia threw sparks that set off an explosion. Both trains caught fire and at least 500 passengers were killed. In 2004, an explosion at a liquefied natural gas (LNG) plant in Algeria killed 27 workers. Natural gas appliances must be regularly checked and serviced to make sure that they do not give off deadly carbon monoxide gas.

Chilling Gas

Natural gas can also be stored and transported as a liquid called liquefied natural gas (LNG). When gas is cooled to -260°F (-162°C), it becomes a liquid and takes up 600 times less space. LNG can be transported long distances in spherical steel containers on tankers. Heating the LNG turns it back into gas.

A tanker's containers are filled with liquefied natural gas at a terminal.

Generating Electricity

We consume more energy from fossil fuels than from all other energy sources put together. Coal, oil, and gas make up more than three-fourths of our primary energy consumption. This means using the fuels directly, by burning them to provide heat or to drive machines such as cars. Fossil fuels are also used to generate two-thirds of the world's electricity, which is called a secondary form of energy.

How the Three Fuels Compare

Coal generates more electricity than any other source. It produces twice as much electricity as natural gas. Many countries depend on coal for electricity (see page 13). Oil produces far less electricity, and hydropower and nuclear power each produce more electricity than oil. The world depends more on fossil fuels for primary energy than on any other energy source. More than one-third of primary energy comes from oil.

What Is a Watt?

A watt (W) is a unit of power that measures the rate of producing or using energy. The term was named after Scottish engineer James Watt (1736–1819), who developed an improved steam engine. Watt measured his engine's performance in horsepower (hp). One horsepower equals 746 watts. Today, watts are generally used to measure electric power.

1 kilowatt (kW) = 1 thousand watts
1 megawatt (MW) = 1 million watts
1 gigawatt (GW) = 1 billion watts

2005	Electricity %	Primary energy %
Coal	40	25
Natural gas	20	21
Oil	7	35
Total	**67**	**81**

How it Came About

In 1831, British scientist Michael Faraday (1791–1867) discovered that he could create electricity by moving a magnet through a coil of copper wire. This process, called electromagnetic induction, led to the invention of the electric generator and electric motor. The world's first coal-fired power station opened in 1882 (see page 13).

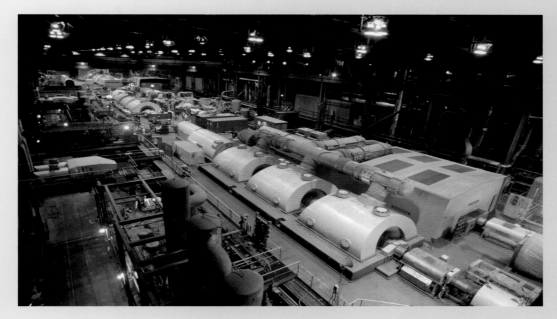

The large generators inside a coal-fired power station are lined up next to each other.

Power stations that burn fossil fuels generate electricity from the movement of a turbine shaft, which is connected to a rotor that makes magnets spin inside wire coils. This turns mechanical energy into electrical energy. The mechanical energy is the power of high-pressure steam, created by burning a fossil fuel to boil water. The steam turns the blades of the turbine.

Largest Coal-Fired Station

This title is claimed by Kendal power station in northeastern South Africa (where 93 percent of electricity comes from coal). The plant was completed in 1993, has six 686 MW generators, and employs 830 workers. Its cooling towers are 541 feet (165 m) tall.

Why Do We Use so Much Coal?

Coal fired the world's first power stations. In many countries, burning coal is a tradition. But the main reason for its popularity today is cost. The South African electricity company Eskom that runs Kendal power station, states: "In South Africa we produce about 34,000 megawatts of electricity to meet current demand, and this figure is growing year by year. The most economical method. . .is to use our abundant supplies of low-quality coal in Mpumalanga and the Northern Province, in power stations sited next to the coal deposits. . .Using coal to generate electricity is not ideal because, no matter how carefully it is burnt, there are gaseous and solid emissions. The gases that are given off include sulfur dioxide, carbon dioxide, and oxides of nitrogen, the first two of which are regarded as having climate change effects on the environment. [see pages 34–35] Unfortunately, coal is the most economical way available to us—all other methods are either impracticable or much more expensive."

Inside a Coal-Fired Power Plant

When a power plant burns coal, it releases energy that has been locked underground for millions of years. This is what happens:

1. A pulverizer crushes lumps of coal into fine powder.
2. The powdered coal is mixed with hot air and blown at high pressure into a boiler or combustion chamber, where it burns.
3. Water flowing through the boiler turns into steam that passes into a superheater where its temperature and pressure increase rapidly.
4. High-pressure steam is piped to the turbine, turning the blades.
5. Water returns to the boiler reheater.
6. The reheated steam is passed to two other turbines.
7. All three turbines are connected by a shaft to the electric generator.
8. The electricity passes to a transformer that makes it more powerful and easier to transmit along power cables.
9. Back in the plant, the used steam turns back into water in a condenser and is returned to the boiler.
10. The water that has absorbed the steam's heat in the condenser is sprayed inside a large cooling tower, then pumped back to the condenser.
11. A fan draws exhaust gases into the chimney that go into the atmosphere.

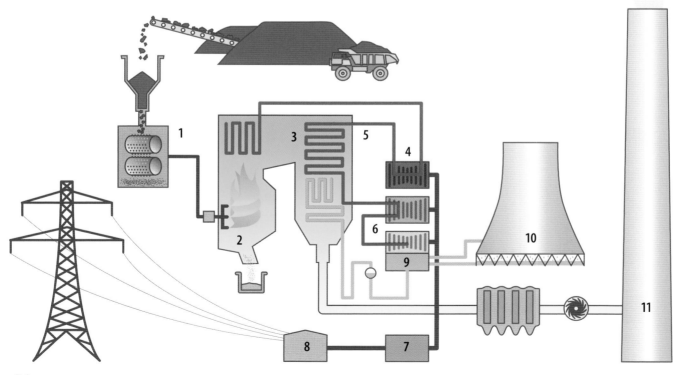

Cooling towers give off water vapor at the Jänschwalde coal-fired power plant in eastern Germany. The plant burns about 88,000 tons (80,000 t) of lignite every day to produce 500 MW of electricity from each of its six generators.

Moving to the Source

During much of the twentieth century, fossil-fueled electric power plants were built in or near cities, to be close to their customers. More recently, plants have been built closer to their source of fuel. Many are near coal mines, while others are close to ports and sources of water.

Are Cooling Towers Harmful?

A survey by the British Royal Society of Chemistry showed that two-thirds of people think that cooling towers emit smoke or carbon dioxide, adding to the greenhouse effect (see page 38). In fact, the towers emit water vapor. Without this, the plants would use enormous amounts of water. They would also release heated water into lakes, rivers, and seas, causing thermal pollution that harms plants and animals. However, cooling towers do send water vapor into the atmosphere, which might be a concern as it is a powerful greenhouse gas (see page 38).

The U.S. National Oceanic and Atmospheric Administration says: "As yet, though the basics of the hydrological cycle are fairly well understood, we have very little comprehension of the complexity of the feedback loops. Also, while we have good atmospheric measurements of other key greenhouse gases, such as carbon dioxide and methane, we have poor measurements of global water vapor, so it is not certain by how much atmospheric concentrations have risen in recent decades or centuries, though satellite measurements, combined with balloon data and some in-situ ground measurements indicate generally positive trends in global water vapor."

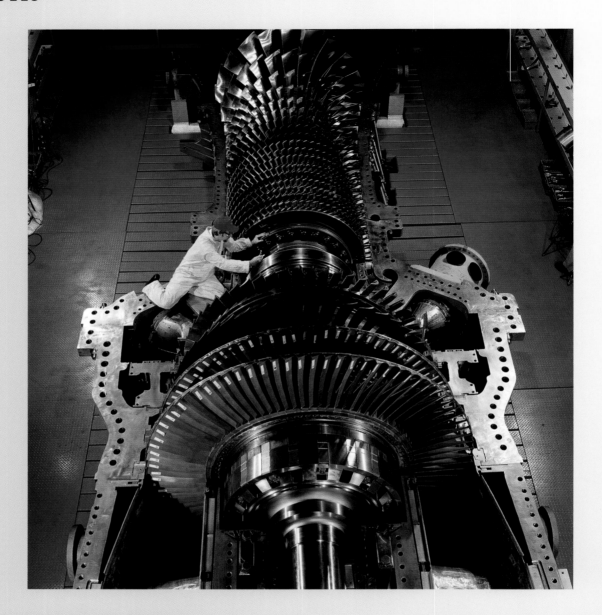

Burning Oil and Gas

Some power stations burn oil or natural gas instead
of coal to fire the boiler and boil water to create steam.
After that stage, the process is the same for all three
fossil fuels. Other plants have gas turbines, which use
the pressure of flowing gases (instead of steam) to turn
the blades of the turbine directly. The gases are created
by burning natural gas or fuel oil (a refined form of
petroleum) in a stream of compressed air. The higher the

*An engineer checks part
of a new gas turbine
at a factory in South
Carolina.*

Which Fossil Fuel Is Best for Electricity?

Environmentalists would rather ask: "Which fossil fuel is least bad?" Coal costs the least, but the new combined-cycle technology makes gas much more efficient so it can compete with coal. The situation constantly changes as the price of coal, oil, and natural gas changes. Oil has become very expensive in recent years. The best fuel for the environment is natural gas.

Scientist James Lovelock writes: "Natural gas in many ways seems an almost ideal fossil fuel and it is used to produce electricity in gas turbine power plants that are compact, highly efficient, and can be built in or near centers of population where they are a combined source of heat and power. . .For the same energy output as from coal or oil, methane combustion releases only half as much carbon dioxide. . .But methane is still a cause for concern."

CCGT systems (see below) are becoming more popular. In the United States, the amount of coal burned to generate electricity has dropped from 52.1 to 49 percent in 10 years. Over the same period, natural gas increased from 13.2 to 20 percent.

pressure, the better the mixture of fuel and air burns. The burning gases expand very quickly, forcing their way into the turbine and spinning the blades.

Gas turbines create higher temperatures than steam turbines—1994°F (1090°C) or higher—and the turbine becomes more efficient as it gets hotter. Most gas turbines use their hot exhaust gases. Some are circulated to a device called a regenerator, where the gases warm compressed air before it enters the combustion chamber. This reduces the amount of fuel needed for combustion.

Combining Gas and Steam

Combined cycle gas turbine (CCGT) plants have both a gas turbine fired by natural gas and a steam turbine powered by the exhaust from the gas turbine. This combination increases the overall efficiency of the plant. Most new gas-fired power plants in North America and Europe are the CCGT type.

Changing Fuels

Ballylumford power station was built near Larne in Northern Ireland in 1943 and powered by coal. In 1974, it was replaced by an oil-fired plant. In 1996, the power station was converted to run on natural gas supplied through an 84 mile (135 km) pipeline from Scotland. In 2003, a new 600 MW CCGT plant was built. This allows the plant to generate 40 percent more electricity using the same amount of gas.

Driving and Flying

Coal and natural gas are the main fossil fuels used to generate electricity, but, for transport, oil is the clear winner. More than a fifth of the world's primary energy is used for transport, followed by industry, construction, and agriculture. Much is in the form of gasoline, of which we burn nearly 792.5 million gallons (3 billion L) every day.

More than 343.4 million gallons (1.3 billion L) (or two-fifths) of petroleum is used by the United States, the world's biggest consumer of oil. The United States has more road vehicles than any other country—765 passenger cars for every thousand people.

Fuel Guzzlers

The top seven oil consumers use more than half of the world's total, and the United States uses more than one-fourth. Compare the figures in the fuel column.

Country	World oil consumption %	World fuel consumption %
USA	25.9	45.0
China	8.6	12.8
Japan	6.7	16.0
Russia	3.6	8.8
Germany	3.3	9.6
India	3.0	2.8
Canada	2.9	14.4
South Korea	2.7	2.4
Brazil	2.6	4.0
Mexico	2.6	8.8
Saudi Arabia	2.5	4.0

Powering the American Dream

Some facts about fuel from the American Petroleum Institute:

"Gasoline: Gasoline helps power the American dream, giving us the freedom to travel where we want and when we want —for work, for school, or for recreation. A steady supply of clean-burning gasoline is central to our nation's economy.

Diesel: Seventy percent of the nation's goods are transported in diesel-powered vehicles, helping to make it America's primary commercial fuel."

America burns nearly half of the world's gasoline. The photograph shows heavy traffic in Atlanta, Georgia.

Rudolf Diesel's Invention

In 1893, German engineer Rudolf Diesel (1853–1913) built his first car engine, which was named after him. Today, most large trucks (as well as ships and many locomotives), vans, and many cars run on diesel fuel. This is a denser form of refined petroleum (oil) fuel. Diesel vehicles can travel a greater distance on a tank of fuel, making it more economical. Diesel-powered vehicles also emit less carbon dioxide. They give off more sulfur than gasoline, but this has been reduced in recent years.

Can We Run Cars on Other Fuels?

Many other fuels have been tried. Early car inventors experimented with steam engines. In 1876, German engineer Nikolaus Otto built a car engine that ran on coal gas. Nine years later, Karl Benz built a three-wheeler that ran on benzene, a form of petroleum. By then, electric cars had already been tried and are still used today. The electricity has to be generated from another energy source, including fossil fuels. Biofuels, such as ethanol, are popular in some countries, including Brazil and Sweden. Perhaps the most interesting development is hydrogen-powered fuel cells that generate electricity to run vehicles. All that is needed are hydrogen and oxygen, with water as a harmless by-product. The problem is that it takes a lot of energy to split hydrogen from water or hydrocarbons.

Jet Engines

A jet engine is a form of gas turbine (see page 29). The engine draws in air at the front, and a compressor raises its pressure. The compressed air is sprayed with jet fuel and the mixture is lit by an electric spark. The burning gases expand and blast out through the back of the engine. This thrusts the aircraft forward through the air.

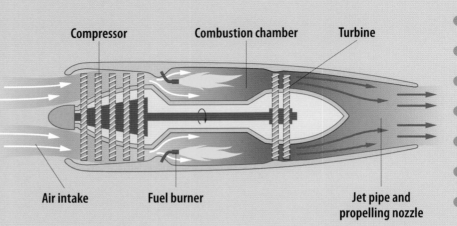

Compressor **Combustion chamber** **Turbine**

Air intake **Fuel burner** **Jet pipe and propelling nozzle**

Fuel for Flight

Jet aircraft burn a refined form of petroleum often called kerosene. Some jets are powered by a mixture of gasoline, kerosene, and other fuels. As flying has increased over the years, the amount of jet fuel produced and consumed has also grown enormously. The United States produces about 27 million barrels of kerosene and 435 million barrels of kerosene-type jet fuels each year. This is about one-sixth of all the oil the United States produces.

The worldwide figure will continue to rise as the number of air passengers is increasing by about 6 percent every year. In 2002, the number of flights was about 3.5 billion. By 2006, this had increased to 4.4 billion. By 2020, the figure could more than double.

Aircraft are parked at southern Germany's Munich airport. In 2007, the airport handled 34 million passengers—10 percent more than in 2006.

Passenger Traffic

The following figures show how the numbers of scheduled air passengers have grown in recent years (by 81 percent in 13 years). The figures are shown in billions of passenger-miles (km), which is the number of passengers multiplied by the distance they flew. Travel experts say the biggest increases were in tourism.

	1993		2006		% increase
North America	505.7 miles	(813.8 km)	778.0 miles	(1,252.1 km)	+ 54%
Europe	309.5 miles	(498.1 km)	594.4 miles	(956.6 km)	+ 92%
Asia/Pacific	273.5 miles	(440.1 km)	581.5 miles	(935.9 km)	+ 113%
Latin America/Caribbean	59.5 miles	(95.7 km)	96.8 miles	(155.8 km)	+ 63%
Middle East	36.3 miles	(58.4 km)	89.0 miles	(143.3 km)	+ 145%
Africa	26.9 miles	(43.3 km)	47.3 miles	(76.2 km)	+ 76%
World total	**1,211.4 miles**	**(1,949.4 km)**	**2,187.0 miles**	**(3,519.9 km)**	**+ 81%**

Into the Atmosphere

The difference between air travel and other forms of transport is that aircraft burn their fuel high in the atmosphere. The exhaust gases that their jet engines emit are even more effective as greenhouse gases at high altitudes. They also emit water vapor, which you see as vapor trails high in the sky. The vapor contributes to an increase in high cloud cover, which has a further blanketing effect on Earth's surface.

Is Air Travel Too Cheap?

Compared with the general cost of living, most airline tickets are much cheaper now than they were in the last century. No one ever wants to pay more than they have to, but many people feel that cheap travel burns too much fossil fuel and increases pollution and global warming. A survey by Cultural Dynamics and Campaign Strategy recorded the following statements:

Air travel is now too cheap	32%
There should be a tax on fuel for air travel	52%
Air travel should be rationed by the government	21%
No more airports should be built	41%
We should limit our air travel voluntarily	59%
There should be a pollution warning on air tickets	61%
Don't know	2%
None of these	12%

What do you think? Which statements do you agree with?

What about the Environment?

Throughout the world, people depend heavily on fossil fuels to provide energy. The biggest disadvantage of this dependence is the effect on the environment. All fossil fuels emit gases when they are burned. These waste gases pollute the atmosphere and contribute to the greenhouse effect that scientists believe causes global warming.

Acid Rain

Acid rain is precipitation that contains dilute forms of substances such as sulfuric acid and nitric acid. Acid rain was first noticed in the middle of the nineteenth century in industrial cities of Britain, and the term was mentioned in a scientific journal in 1859. But concern about acid rain grew during the 1960s, when people noticed that trees were dying so fast that entire forests were at risk. They then realized that this form of pollution damaged forests, lakes, and rivers, harming wildlife and endangering the environment.

The most affected regions of the world were central Europe, Scandinavia, eastern North America, and parts of Asia. When scientists realized that most acid rain was caused by industrial waste gases from burning fossil fuels, they persuaded some governments to bring in measures to reduce emissions. One measure introduced devices called scrubbers, which absorb sulfur dioxide as it passes through factory and power station chimneys.

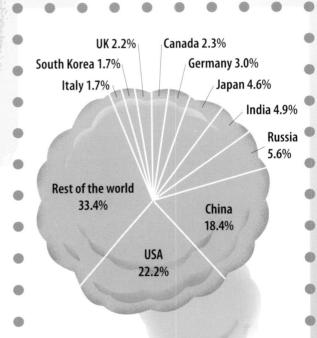

UK 2.2% Canada 2.3%
South Korea 1.7% Germany 3.0%
Italy 1.7% Japan 4.6%
India 4.9%
Russia 5.6%
Rest of the world 33.4%
China 18.4%
USA 22.2%

Biggest Emitters

According to the United Nations, the top four emitting countries produce more than half the world's carbon dioxide (CO_2) emissions. The U.S. Department of State says that CO_2 makes up about 80 percent of total U.S. emissions from fossil fuel combustion.

The effects of pollution can clearly be seen on these trees in Queensland, Australia.

Can We Prevent Fossil-Fuel Pollution?

Yes, by burning fewer fossil fuels! According to the U.S. Environmental Protection Agency, we can all take action as individuals: "It may seem like there is not much that one individual can do to stop acid deposition. However, like many environmental problems, acid deposition is caused by the cumulative actions of millions of individual people. Therefore, each individual can also reduce their contribution to the problem and become part of the solution. Individuals can contribute directly by conserving energy, since energy production causes the largest portion of the acid deposition problem. For example, you can:

• Turn off lights, computers, and other appliances when you're not using them.

• Use energy-efficient appliances: lighting, air conditioners, heaters, refrigerators, washing machines, etc.

• Only use electric appliances when you need them.

• Keep your thermostat at 68°F (20°C) in the winter and 71.6°F (22°C) in the summer. You can turn it even lower in the winter and higher in the summer when you are away from home.

• Insulate your home as best you can.

• Carpool, use public transportation, or better yet, walk or bicycle whenever possible.

• Buy vehicles with low emissions and properly maintain your vehicle.

• Be well informed."

Mining at the Top of the World...

Fossil fuels present another danger to the environment. People are looking for new sources, and this has led them to the last two great wildernesses of the world—the polar regions.

In 1998, the U.S. Geological Survey studied the northern region of the Arctic National Wildlife Refuge and found that there may be as much as 11.8 billion barrels of recoverable oil in the area.

In 2005, the U.S. government was about to give the go-ahead for oil exploration when a group of senators changed the bill. The refuge area is close to the Prudhoe Bay oil fields that have been worked since 1968, but environmentalists argue that this is one of the last

A fox cub leaves its den in the Arctic National Wildlife Refuge. The region is under threat.

Looking After Wildlife

The U.S. Fish & Wildlife Service explains the point of protection: "The Arctic National Wildlife Refuge was established to preserve unique wildlife, wilderness, and recreational values; to conserve caribou herds, polar bears, grizzly bears, musk ox, dall sheep, wolves, wolverines, snow geese, peregrine falcons, other migratory birds, Dolly Varden, and grayling [both trout-like fish]; to fulfill international treaty obligations; to provide opportunities for continued subsistence uses; and to ensure necessary water quality and quantity...The 19.2 million acre (77,700 sq km) Arctic National Wildlife Refuge supports the greatest variety of plant and animal life of any park or refuge in the circumpolar Arctic...Eight million acres (32,400 sq km) of the Arctic Refuge are designated wilderness."

Do We Need International Agreements on Mining Rights?

We do and they already exist, but countries constantly look for ways to get around agreements or break them. In 1996, eight Arctic nations—Canada, Denmark (for Greenland), Finland, Iceland, Norway, Russia, Sweden, and the United States (for Alaska)—formed an Arctic Council to protect their environment. The council represents about 4 million people, including the Aleut, Inuit, and Sami peoples. One of its plans aims to limit and reduce emissions of pollutants into the Arctic. The continent around the South Pole is covered by the Antarctic Treaty of 1961, which originally had 12 member nations and now has 46. The treaty allows people to use Antarctica only for peaceful purposes, such as scientific research. In 1991, extra environmental protection was added, banning all activities relating to mineral resources (including fossil fuels) except for scientific research.

The Amundsen-Scott Research Station at the South Pole was built in 1975.

unspoiled regions of the world, which is why it was made a refuge in the first place.

...and at the Bottom of the World

In 2007, Britain announced that it was planning to apply to the United Nations for more than 386,000 square miles (1 million sq km) of seabed off the coast of Antarctica. This is the world's only uninhabited continent, home to just a small number of scientists. Much of the seabed where the British want to drill is so deep that it is not yet technically possible to extract oil and gas, but Britain and other nations are looking to the future, when oil becomes scarce. Environmentalists are concerned about this and point out that we know very little about these deep waters, where there may be fish species and other sea creatures yet to be discovered.

Adding to the Greenhouse Effect

The biggest disadvantage of fossil fuels (and the largest issue) is the way
in which burning them adds to the greenhouse effect. The atmosphere
prevents some of the Sun's rays from reaching Earth. Its gases also stop
some heat escaping from Earth, just as glass traps warmth inside a
greenhouse. We are adding to this natural greenhouse effect by emitting
so many waste gases from power plants, factories, and cars. Many
greenhouse gases are produced when we burn fossil fuels—especially
carbon dioxide.

Glacier ice melts and falls into a lake at a national park in Argentina.

Alarming Climate Changes

Scientists call the changes brought about by human use of fossil fuels the enhanced
greenhouse effect. They are concerned about this effect because of the ways in
which global warming is changing our world. The 2007 report by the UN's
Intergovernmental Panel on Climate Change (IPCC) reported that:

- world temperatures could increase by 1.98°F to 11.52°F (1.1°C to 6.4°C)
  this century;
- sea levels will probably increase by 7 to 23 inches (18 to 59 cm) by 2100;
- it is 90 percent certain that there will be more frequent heat waves and heavy
  rainfall; and
- it is 66 percent certain that there will be more droughts and hurricanes.

Fossil Fuels to Blame

According to IPCC's 2007 report: "Carbon dioxide is the most important anthropogenic [resulting from human activity] greenhouse gas. The global atmospheric concentration of carbon dioxide has increased from a preindustrial value of about 280 ppm [parts per million] to 379 ppm in 2005… The annual carbon dioxide concentration growth rate was larger during the last ten years… than it has been since the beginning of continuous direct atmospheric measurement. The primary source of the increased atmospheric concentration of carbon dioxide since the preindustrial period results from fossil fuel use."

Are the Experts Right?

Some people believe the effects of human-caused global warming are exaggerated. Environmentalists call them climate change deniers. You have to form your own opinion, but remember that the IPCC is a scientific body established by the World Meteorological Organization and the United Nations Environment Programme, with experts from more than 130 countries and more than 2,500 scientific reviewers. The organization shared the 2007 Nobel Peace Prize with Al Gore (who starred in the Oscar-winning documentary film *An Inconvenient Truth*). They were awarded the prize for "their efforts to build up and disseminate greater knowledge about manmade climate change and to lay the foundations for the measures that are needed to counteract such change." The IPCC say that there is a 5 percent (or 1 in 20) chance that any of their findings or conclusions could be wrong.

HOW DO DIFFERENT FUELS COMPARE?

This chart compares fuels according to the energy and carbon dioxide they produce when burned.

ENERGY
Megajoules per kilogram of fuel

CARBON DIOXIDE
Kilograms per gigajoule of energy

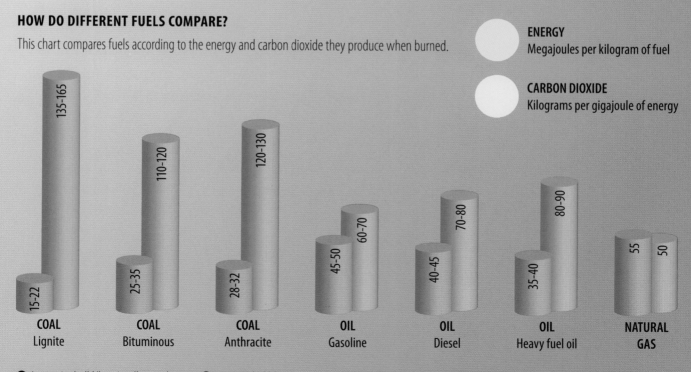

	ENERGY	CARBON DIOXIDE
COAL Lignite	15-22	135-165
COAL Bituminous	25-35	110-120
COAL Anthracite	28-32	120-130
OIL Gasoline	45-50	60-70
OIL Diesel	40-45	70-80
OIL Heavy fuel oil	35-40	80-90
NATURAL GAS	55	50

● 1 megajoule (MJ) = 1 million joules   ● 1 gigajoule (GJ) = 1 thousand million joules   ● A joule is a unit of energy: 1 joule per second equals 1 watt

What Does the Future Hold?

For the foreseeable future, it seems that the amount of coal, oil, and gas we produce and use worldwide will continue to increase. At the same time, scientists are looking for more reserves of fossil fuels, new ways to make stocks last longer, modern technologies to make the fuels less polluting, and new sources of energy.

Clean Coal Technology

The coal industry is working on methods to make coal less polluting. It claims these will help make coal much cleaner in the future. First, coal can be prepared so that it burns more efficiently. One technique involves putting the coal into a fluid so that unwanted material sinks and can be removed. Another method is coal gasification that turns coal into gas. In Integrated Gasification Combined Cycle (IGCC) systems, coal reacts with oxygen and steam to form a syngas, which can be burned in a gas turbine. Waste gases from coal can also be cleaned. Nitrogen oxides can be reduced by using special burners. Sulfur dioxide can be removed by scrubbers (see page 34). Other particles can be removed after burning by using an electrical field to attract them onto collection plates.

Capturing Carbon

Some experts believe that carbon capture and storage (CCS) could make an important difference. The process prevents carbon dioxide (CO_2) from entering the atmosphere by removing it and storing it deep underground. CO_2 can be removed before being burned by a gasification method. Alternatively, it can be removed during the exhaust process by absorbing it into a solvent. The third possibility is to burn the fuel in oxygen instead of air (called oxyfuel combustion) to create a stream of CO_2 that can be removed. The separated CO_2 can be piped underground into disused coal fields, rocks saturated with salt water, or oil pockets where the gas can help build pressure, making extraction easier (see page 19).

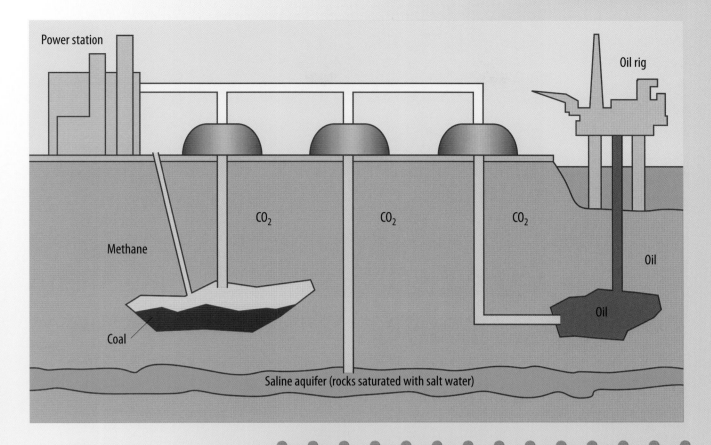

Power station

Oil rig

Methane

CO_2

CO_2

CO_2

Oil

Coal

Oil

Saline aquifer (rocks saturated with salt water)

The diagram shows three options for storing carbon dioxide that has been captured before it leaves the power station. The methane can be used as fuel for the plant.

Can Fossil Fuels Ever Be Clean or Green?

These may be the wrong terms to use, as fossil fuels are by nature "dirty" because of the greenhouse gases they produce. The CCS processes are technically possible but have not yet been used on a large scale because of high costs. Experts think that CCS could reduce CO_2 emissions by up to 90 percent, but it could increase costs by just as much and use more fuel and energy.

Environmental organization Greenpeace says: "Monitoring and verification over decades is necessary to guarantee the retention of the stored carbon dioxide. Even then, opportunities to intervene in order to prevent or control unexpected leakage events are likely to be limited. CCS is not a technology of today nor of the immediate future because of technical uncertainties as to whether it will work or not." The environmentalist George Monbiot has called CCS a "great green scam" and claims that the process would increase carbon emissions 7 to 15 times.

This image from space shows North America lit up at night. We are using more electricity than ever, and we are likely to continue doing so.

Coal Consumption

According to the U.S. Energy Information Administration (EIA), coal's share of world energy consumption will continue to increase until 2030. It stands at about 25 percent now, and its share will increase to more than 28 percent by 2030. Given all the environmental problems, this seems surprising. The main reason is the increasing need for energy as the number of people in the world continues to grow. From 2008 to 2030, world energy consumption may increase by more than 55 percent.

Exploiting Other Fossil Fuels

Scientists and engineers may be able to use what are called nonconventional oils in the future. One possible source is oil shale (or kerogen shale), a sedimentary rock from which oil can be obtained. There are large deposits in Brazil, China, Estonia, Sweden, and the United States, but up to now vast amounts of rock have been needed to produce small quantities of oil. The mined rock is crushed and heated, giving off oil vapors that condense into a liquid.

Another nonconventional source is tar sands (or bituminous sands), which are found in Canada and Venezuela. They are deposits of sand that contain bitumen, which is a heavy form of crude oil. The sand is mixed with hot water and steam, so that the oil floats to the top and then can be heated

Are New Sources the Answer?

This remains to be seen. There may be further discoveries of nonconventional sources to add to oil shale and tar sands. The problems are always the same, however. The oil is difficult and expensive to extract. And the process also uses energy. In terms of mining and greenhouse gases, all fossil fuels inevitably cause environmental problems.

The environmentalist journalist George Monbiot wrote in 2007: "The IEA [International Energy Agency] believes that this crisis will be averted by opening new fields and using unconventional oil. But these cause environmental disasters of their own. Around half the new discoveries the agency expects over the next 25 years will take place in the Arctic or in the very deep sea (between 2000 and 4000 meters). In either case, a major oil spill, in such slow and fragile ecosystems, would be catastrophic. Mining unconventional oil—such as the tar sands in Canada or the kerogen shales in the U.S.—produces far more carbon dioxide than drilling for ordinary petroleum. It also uses and pollutes great volumes of fresh water, and wrecks thousands of acres of pristine land."

to produce oils such as kerosene. Industry experts predict that by 2020 up to 90 percent of Canada's oil production may come from the Athabasca tar sand deposits in Alberta.

Rising Production

The chart shows the Energy Information Administration's prediction of how production of all three fossil fuels will increase. Coal shows the biggest increase during the period (72 percent), followed by gas (64 percent), and oil (40 percent).

Coal production (million metric tons)

Oil production (million barrels per day)

Natural gas production (trillion cubic meters)

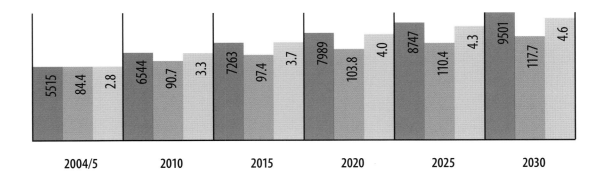

	2004/5	2010	2015	2020	2025	2030
Coal	5515	6544	7263	7989	8747	9501
Oil	84.4	90.7	97.4	103.8	110.4	117.7
Natural gas	2.8	3.3	3.7	4.0	4.3	4.6

Glossary

biofuel   A fuel produced from biomass, such as ethanol from sugar cane.

bitumen   A sticky mixture of hydrocarbons found in tar and similar substances.

butane   A highly flammable gas present in oil and natural gas.

carbon dioxide (CO_2)   A greenhouse gas given off when fossil fuels are burned.

carbon monoxide   A poisonous gas given off when fossil fuels are burned without enough air.

climate change   A change in general weather conditions over a long period of time, including higher temperatures, more or less rain, droughts, etc.

combustion   The burning of fuel.

condense   To change from a gas into a liquid (as steam into water).

cooling tower   A tall structure that cools steam and turns it back to water.

crude oil   Oil (or petroleum) as it is found naturally underground.

derrick   A framework that supports drilling equipment.

diesel (diesel oil)   A fuel obtained from crude oil.

emission   Producing and giving off something (such as a waste gas); also, the waste gas produced and given off.

ethane   A highly flammable gas present in oil and natural gas.

ethanol (ethyl alcohol)   A liquid biofuel that can be produced from plants such as sugar cane and corn.

gasoline   A fuel refined from oil.

global warming   Heating up of Earth's surface, especially caused by pollution from burning fossil fuels.

greenhouse effect   Warming of Earth's surface caused especially by pollution from burning fossil fuels.

hydrocarbon   A chemical compound containing hydrogen and carbon.

hydrogen   A light, colorless gas that combines with oxygen to make water.

impermeable   Does not let liquid or gas through.

impurities   Small quantities of substances that make another substance less pure.

Industrial Revolution   The rapid development of machinery, factories, and industry that began in the late eighteenth century.

kerosene   A fuel oil made by distilling petroleum.

methane   A flammable gas that is the main element in natural gas.

nonrenewable energy   Energy that is used up and cannot be replaced (from sources such as coal, gas, oil, or uranium).

octane   A liquid hydrocarbon in oil; high-quality gasoline has more octane.

pentane   A highly flammable liquid present in oil and natural gas.

piston   A cylinder that is pushed up and down inside an engine.

propane   A highly flammable gas present in oil and natural gas.

renewable energy   Sources of energy that do not run out by being used, such as biomass, geothermal, solar, water, and wind.

sedimentary rock   Rock that formed from layers of sediment (material worn away from other rocks) on the ocean floor.

solvent   A liquid in which substances are dissolved.

sulfur dioxide (SO_2)   A poisonous gas given off by burning coal.

thermal pollution   Environmental damage caused by heat.

turbine   A machine with rotating blades that turn a shaft.

valve   A device that opens and closes a pipe to control flow.

water vapor   Water in the form of a gas.

Web Sites

Oil and Gas Information from the American Petroleum Institute
www.api.org

Coal Facts and New Technologies from the World Coal Institute
www.worldcoal.org

Natural Gas and Liquefied Natural Gas (LNG)
www.naturalgas.org

Questions and Answers on Greenhouse Gases from the U.S. National Oceanic and Atmospheric Administration
http://lwf.ncdc.noaa.gov/oa/climate/gases.html#wv

Greenpeace's Views on "Dirty Energy"
www.greenpeace.org/seasia/en/asia-energy-revolution/dirty-energy

Index